35 GREAT CHILDREN'S LESSONS

THAT BRING THE BIBLE TO LIFE

All Rights Reserved
Mark J Musser Books
2016

Special Thanks To:

God for guiding my steps and for my wife and son who put up with my missteps

Scriptures cited are from: *Holy Bible. New Living Translation copyright© 1996, 2004, 2007, 2013 by Tyndale House Foundation. Used by permission of Tyndale House Publishers Inc., Carol Stream, Illinois 60188. All rights reserved.*

PARENTING BOOKS BY MARK J MUSSER

50 Great Object Lessons that Bring the Bible to Life

50 More Great Object Lessons that Bring the Bible to Life

When it comes to explaining the Bible to children and pre-teens, many parents and even Sunday school teachers are at loss as to how to really connect their children or students to God's Word, bringing it to life in interesting and creative ways. Thankfully, 50 Great Object Lessons makes it incredibly easy!

Lessons on Parenting: What Parents in the Bible Can Teach Parents Today

The Bible is full of insightful and meaningful narratives where Moms and Dads are found making choices that impact their children and those around them. The blessings or fallout from those choices and decisions most definitely can apply to our lives as parents today.

The Christ Centered Home: Turning Your Kids into Christ-Centered Disciples

Long before God established the nation of Israel to be His chosen people, and long before He established the church to spread His glory, He established the family to be the primary means of making disciples. Is your family fulfilling that mandate?

Parenting Essentials: 10 Things Every Parent Should Do

Do you know what you should be doing as a Christian parent? Do you understand what essential characteristics must be modeled for your children and teens? These are the questions this family-defining book seeks to answer.

OTHER BOOKS BY MARK J MUSSER

Answers for the Afterlife: The Truth about Heaven and Your Place in It
Is there life after death? If so, where is it and how do I get there? These questions leave us uneasy. Instead of living in assurance, we spend our days doubting the afterlife or wondering where we'll end up when we die. But we can be sure. Are you?

World Changer: Impact the World for Christ Starting Now
Do you want to be a world changer, impacting our planet one needy soul at a time? This book will inspire you to make a difference and step beyond the ordinary. Don't miss your chance to leave a legacy for Christ. Don't miss the adventure of a lifetime.

Finding the True You: Discover Who You Were Created to Be
"Who am I, and what is my purpose?" If you are looking for the answers to these foundational questions, download a copy of this book today!

Searching for More: Finding the Fulfillment You Long For
The answers to fulfillment and satisfaction are not found in anything this world has to offer. They are found in Christ alone. Discover what you're missing!

Check out these titles, and find free resources, at www.markjmusser.com

TABLE OF THEMES

Introduction

INTRODUCTION

God's plan from the beginning has been incredibly simple. The current generation of Christians must teach the next generation of Christians what it means to follow Christ. Then, when that generation grows up, they will turn around and do the same for those who follow.

That is the purpose of this lesson book. Let it be a tool in your hands to help disciple and train the next generation to live for, and serve, Jesus Christ. Whether it be in your home, in Children's Church, Sunday school, Pioneer Clubs, AWANA, tweens ministry, or some other avenue, I pray God will work mightily through you!

Each lesson is broken down into the R.E.A.D. F.F. formula. The "R" stands for READ. Right at the beginning of each lesson, you will share a Scripture passage with the children.

"E" stands for ENGAGE. Here you will share a short story or anecdote.

What follows is "A" where you will ASK a series of questions designed to get the children to think about, and interact with, the lesson and the Scripture.

"D," for DO, comes next. Here is where you work to etch the lesson onto the hearts and minds of those in your care as you go through an object lesson, craft, or exercise together.

The final two "F's" stand for FOLLOW UP and FINISH UP. As you near the end of each lesson, you will follow up with questions and application ideas to check on what has been retained and to encourage the children to put into action what they just learned about.

Finally, you will finish up with a time of prayer.

As a parent or teacher, God has called you to the great task of discipleship. Grab hold of that responsibility and watch as the Lord does awesome things in and through you!

Well, what are you waiting for? Let the adventure begin!

LESSON 1

SUPPLIES
Paper doll cut outs , crayons or colored pencils, scissors, tape or stapler

READ: 2 Corinthians 5:17

ENGAGE
Mason Crosby was six years old when he went into foster care. His mother had died suddenly, and his dad had many problems. For almost four years, he was in one foster home after another. It was not an easy life. Sure, he was with caring families, but he had no one around that he could call "Mom and Dad."

Then, one day, it happened. The Sampsell family wanted to adopt Mason. Over the next six months, he met with this family many times—going out to eat, playing ball, and spending the night a few times. Soon, this loving family officially adopted him, and Mason Crosby became Mason Sampsell.

Did you know that when we accept Jesus into our hearts something similar happens? We get a new identity. We are adopted into the family of God, become known as Christians, and should start living our lives in a whole new way.

ASK
What was Mason sad about in our story?

What do you think life would be like without a Mom or Dad to love and care for you?

What do you think our Bible verse for today means when it says God makes us into new people when we accept Jesus?

What should change after you become part of Jesus' family?

Who do you know that is *not* part of Jesus' family? List three to five people below:

DO
- Have paper doll cut-outs prepared (or use the one provided in Appendix – A) and hand one to each child
- Explain that when we accept Jesus, we join together with many, many others to become part of God's family
- Each child is going to use the paper doll cut-out to draw him or herself—same color hair and eyes, wearing a favorite outfit, etc.
- After each child is finished coloring, you will take all the cut-outs and join them together by the "hands" with tape or staples into a long string of paper dolls
- Using tape or wall-putty hang them on the wall

FOLLOW UP
Ask: We know that it is super-great to be adopted by God and to become part of His family, but do you know what it takes to be adopted by God?

Share with the children how when we admit that we have sinned and believe that God sent His Son to die on the cross for our sins, then we can be part of God's family

You may want to ask if anyone has never admitted their sin and trusted in Jesus. This would be a great time to see another child adopted into God's family!

FINISH UP
- Pray and thank God for adopting you into His family
- Pray for those you listed under the last question in the "ASK" section of the lesson

LESSON 2

SUPPLIES
Picture of a butterfly, picture of a caterpillar, colored pens or pencils, glue, construction paper, scissors

READ: 2 Corinthians 5:15-17

ENGAGE
The Smith's had a small, old TV in their living room that did not work very well. One day, a neighbor saw this poor little TV and promised to get the Smith's a new one the next week. When next week came, seven year-old Bobby and nine year-old Susie were super-excited to see something gift-wrapped in their living room. They knew it had to be that new TV, so they quickly tore off the wrapping paper just to find that is was their same old TV—only it had been painted white by their neighbor!

The Smith's complained to their neighbor about this, but he told them that it was new because it looks different on the *outside*. Bobby and Susie were not very happy about this and tried to explain to their neighbor that just because something looks different on the outside that doesn't make it "new."

ASK
How did the neighbor make the Smith's TV "new"?

Why was the TV really NOT made new?

What would you think if one of your neighbors did this to your family?

Sometimes, when people accept Jesus, they just work really hard to make the outside look good without letting Jesus change the inside—how is that like painting an old TV to look new?

What does our Bible verse say about this?

What does it mean to be changed on the inside?

DO
- Print out a picture of a caterpillar.
- Print out a picture of a butterfly.
- Show the kids the picture of the caterpillar you printed and explain that you are now going to make this caterpillar brand new
- Proceed to recolor it with a marker, pen, crayon, or colored pencil
- Ask your children if you really just made this caterpillar new
- Next, show the picture of the butterfly

FOLLOW UP
Explain that this butterfly is actually the new "caterpillar" that has been transformed from the inside out into a new creature

Share how when we accept Jesus, we need to let Him change us *completely* from the inside out

FINISH UP
- Pray and thank Jesus that He can do great things in you
- Pray and give the children a chance to tell God about something that needs to change in their lives

LESSON 3

SUPPLIES
OPTION 1--Remote control car, blindfold

OPTION 2--A bunch of objects to strew on the floor, blindfold(s)

READ: Galatians 2:19 & 20

ENGAGE
Ten year-old Joey and his dad loved to play the Nintendo game *Super Mario Brothers 3* together. In this game, two players can work side by side to beat levels and save the princess. The only problem with this game is that each player only gets a couple lives. Many times, young Joey would run out of lives to play, and Dad would be playing by himself. Trying to be a good example, Joey's dad would often hand over his controller and say, "Here Joey, you can have my lives."

Doing that one day, Joey's dad was reminded that this is what Jesus wants us to do with Him. He wants us to hand over the controller for our lives and say to Him, "Here Jesus, you can control my life."

ASK
What nice thing would Joey's dad do for him while they were playing video games?

One day, while doing this, what did Joey's dad think about?

What do our Bible verses say about who we should be living for?

What do you think it means to give God control of your life?

Have you given Jesus the controller for your life? If not, why not?

Why is it important that you let Jesus have control of your life?

DO—OPTION 1
- If you have a remote control vehicle, put a blindfold on a child and have him or her work to control this vehicle without being able to see
- Next, take the blindfold off and have the children control the vehicle being able to see everything

DO—OPTION 2
- If you do not have a remote control vehicle, try this instead
- Blindfold a child (or children) and then strew a bunch of items across the floor
- Tell the child(ren) to get from one end of the room to the other without touching any of the items
- When it proves impossible, let him or her try without the blindfold

FOLLOW UP
Ask: Which was easier? With the blindfold or without the blindfold?

Discuss how we don't know as much as God does. He can see everything—even the future. We need to give Him control because He can do a better job at "directing" our lives

FINISH UP
- Pray and thank Jesus that He died for your sins and made a way for you to have eternal life
- Pray and give the children a chance to tell Jesus that He can have control of their lives and use them to do great things for Him

LESSON 4

SUPPLIES
CD-player with plug

READ: John 15:1-8

ENGAGE
Jordan was so excited! His parents had finally bought a Wii U. He had been begging for one since it first came out, and now it was here.

He quickly ripped open the box and started setting everything up. He plugged the cables into the back of the TV, set up the sensor bar, put batteries in the controllers, and hooked them up. Oh boy, was he ready to play!

Though when he went to start *Super Mario Bros U*, nothing seemed to be happening at all. Jordan thought for sure that the Wii was defective, but when Dad checked it out, he noticed something Jordan forgot to do—plug the power cord into the outlet.

You certainly can't play the Wii on the TV without it being connected to a power source. And, we certainly can't do too much if we are not connected to God—the greatest power source in the universe!

ASK
Jordan thought he had done everything he needed to do to play the Wii, but what did he forget to do?

Have you ever thought something was broken, but then discovered it just wasn't plugged in or the batteries were missing?

What are some things you can only use if they are plugged into a power source?

In verse 5 of our Bible passage, what does Jesus say is possible for us to do if we are not connected to Him?

What are things we can all do to stay daily connected to Jesus?

DO

- Have a CD player with you that is unplugged
- After finishing the last question above, tell your family (class) that you'd like to play a special song for everyone
- As you go to do so, ask a child to hit the play button
- When it doesn't come on, see if your child connects the non-working CD-player with the lesson and checks the power outlet

FOLLOW UP

After the problem has been discovered, discuss again how the CD-player can't really do anything without being connected to a power source. Likewise, we need to be daily connected to God to do great things

Brainstorm ideas of what you can all do to stay connected the Lord. Have the class commit to doing at least one of those things each day

FINISH UP

- Pray and thank God for having all the power you need for life
- Pray and ask God to help you stay connected to Him at all times

LESSON 5

SUPPLIES
Washable markers, access to sink or tub (or have wet-wipes handy)

READ: John 8:1-11

ENGAGE
School was just about to start and fifth grader Jason was *not* excited about going back at all! It wasn't that he didn't like school—it was okay enough. It was because, over Christmas break, he was caught stealing candy from a store, and *lots* of people heard all about it.

He thought for sure that when school started, everyone would be staring at him and whispering, "There's that kid who got caught stealing and even the police showed up!" Jason could hardly stand the thought, so he was already planning ways to fake he was sick so he wouldn't have to go.

Perhaps you have felt like Jason before. You did something bad, people found out about it, and you were embarrassed by all the stares and whispers. Well, guess what? With Jesus, you can be forgiven. You don't have worry about what everyone else thinks! Jesus loves you and wants to forgive you!

ASK
What did Jason do that made him NOT want to go to school?

What is an embarrassing thing you have done?

What did the people in our Bible story want to do with the woman they caught doing a bad thing?

What did Jesus do with her?

Jesus forgave her, but what command did he give her in verse 11? Why is it important to make good choices after being forgiven?

DO
- Have washable markers handy
- Talk to your children (class) about different kinds of sin—have them give examples of sinning by word, sinning by deed, and sinning by thought
- As each child gives examples, write each one down on their arms. Soon all arms will be "covered in sin"
- Discuss how we all do many sinful things and it covers us with sin. But when we ask Jesus for forgiveness, He comes and cleanses (washes) our sin away, leaving NO trace

FOLLOW UP
Take each child to a sink or tub (or have a wet-wipes handy) and wash away "the sin"

Finish by stating that we don't need to be continually embarrassed or ashamed of what we did in the past. If we asked for forgiveness, no trace is left. It is gone!

FINISH UP
- Pray and thank God for His great forgiveness and love
- Pray and give the children a chance to ask God to forgive them for any sins they have done and then ask for the strength to make better choices

LESSON 6

SUPPLIES
Tea cups, napkins, crown template

READ: Matthew 5:19

ENGAGE
If you were born into the royal family in England, you would have been taught from day one the "proper" way to act. You would have learned such things as: A woman must always be seen with a hat on her head. A man must always sleep in full length pajamas. You should not touch a banister unless you are wearing white gloves. Females must greet other royalty with a low, sweeping curtsy, while males must greet other royalty with a bow at the waist. The handle of a tea-cup is grasped by the thumb and forefinger with the pinky extended. And the list goes on.

The point is if you are royalty in England, you are expected to act like it. Likewise, as children of God (princes and princesses of the Kingdom of Heaven), you are royalty as well. So, you must act like it.

ASK
Do you think any of the "proper" ways for royalty in England to act is a bit strange? If so, why?

What does Jesus say in our Bible verse for today?

Why is it important for the children of God to obey Him?

Where are you struggling to live like a prince or princess of God?

DO
- Have the kids practice some of the requirements of English royalty—the

bow, the curtsy, the proper holding of the tea cup, etc.

- You may even want to have tea "as royalty." Have fancy hats available (or create your own crowns by using the crown template in Appendix - B), use "high language," drink with the pinky extended, napkins on the lap, etc.

FOLLOW UP

Ask: What are some ways that we can practice the requirements of Heavenly royalty like loving others, serving others, honoring God, being thankful, etc.?

Ask: Which ones will you try this week?

FINISH UP

- Pray and thank God for making you His child
- Pray and ask God to help you all live in a way that pleases Him and shows the world how awesome He is

LESSON 7

SUPPLIES
Quarters, clue sheets, and a "treasure" like a bag of candy

READ: Matthew 13:44-46

ENGAGE
King Edward VIII of England was only king for less than a year. However, this did not bother Edward at all because he did *not* like being king. There was too much responsibility, and he wanted to just have fun. In fact, King Edward was doing such a bad job as king that government officials stopped sending him documents because they knew he would do nothing with them.

Even though England was close to war with Germany, Edward spent more time on cruise ships than doing work. Finally, Edward gave up being king and his younger brother Albert was crowned the new King of England.

To be royalty is a great responsibility and it requires a great deal of hard work and dedication. King Edward did not want to do it. I hope that you are willing to give your all for God's Kingdom!

ASK
If God is King, and we are adopted as His children, what does that make us?

How do you think a prince or princess in God's kingdom should act?

What do you think about how King Edward was acting?

In our Bible verses, what did the people give up to get the treasure and the pearl?

Jesus is saying that we need to be willing to give up everything for the Kingdom of Heaven. What would be hard for you to give up?

What can help you be the best prince or princess you can be?

DO

- Hide something you know the children will really like, such as a bag of candy
- Be prepared to distribute around four to six quarters between the children. For example, if you have four children, you can give them each one quarter
- Prepare clues equal to the amount of quarters you distribute. For example, if you have given out four quarters, prepare four clues
- Tell the kids that you have hidden something fantastic. To find it, however, they will need clues. And each clue will cost a quarter
- Have a child give you one quarter to get the first clue. After they all discover that initial clue, have another child give you a quarter for the next clue, and so on
- In the end, they will need to give up *all* their quarters to get the "treasure"
- One way to do this is as follows: Get the quarter for the first clue which will say: "Go to where we keep our towels." Your kids will wander to the towel closet. In that closet, you will have placed a paper which says, "Give a quarter to get the next clue." That clue can read: "How many cans of soup do we have? Go and find out." When the kids get to where you keep the soup, on top of one of the cans can be the next paper which says, "Give a quarter to get the next clue"
- Have enough clues for each quarter. The last clue, then, will lead to the "treasure"

FOLLOW UP
Ask: Why were you willing to give up all the quarters?

Go on to discuss with the children how they were willing to give up *all* their quarters to get the treasure because they knew something way better than quarters was waiting for them

Share how God wants us to be willing to give up everything to have His treasure—eternal life in Heaven

FINISH UP
- Pray and thank God for being part of His Kingdom
- Pray and ask God to help everyone be the best prince or princess they can be

LESSON 8

SUPPLIES
Pictures of things clearly sticking out and a "Where's Waldo?" picture

READ: Philippians 1:27

ENGAGE
Abbie was ten years-old when her parents moved to Romania to be missionaries. When they got off the plane at the airport, Abbie noticed lots of people looking at them. "Why are so many people staring at us Daddy?" She asked.

"Well," Dad started, "We do talk differently than they do, and we are dressed differently too. We kind of stick out!"

Abbie didn't really like the fact that they "stuck out," but Dad thought it was a great time for a lesson. "You know," Dad continued. "Really, as Christians, we should be sticking out anyway. We should be living as citizens of heaven. That means we should be acting different from the rest of the world."

Abbie smiled as Mom chimed in, "Hopefully, in a couple months, we'll only be sticking out because we are Christians, not because we are Americans!"

ASK
What was Abbie noticing everyone was doing? Why did this bother her?

If you could visit any country in the world, where would it be?

How does our Bible verse say we should be living?

What does it mean to live like a citizen of Heaven?

Does your family "stick out" because you are living like that?

What are the good things, and the bad things, about "sticking out"?

DO

- Go to an image search engine like *Google* or *Bing* and type in "sticking out in a crowd." Choose a few pictures to print out or display for your kids that show items quite clearly sticking out
- Next type in "Where's Waldo" and choose a picture or two to display
- Show the first set of pictures and have the kids choose the item or color that is clearly sticking out
- Next, pull out the "Where's Waldo" pictures and have your kids attempt to find Waldo
- It should prove *much more* difficult to find Waldo than it did to find the items that stuck out in the previous set of pictures

FOLLOW UP

Ask: Why is it important to "stick out for Jesus" and not blend in like Waldo does?

Discuss how we need to stick out for Jesus, so people can see Him in us. If we blend in with the world, no one will meet Jesus and have their lives changed forever

FINISH UP

- Pray and thank God that Jesus made a way for you to become a Christian and a citizen of Heaven
- Pray and ask God to help each of you live in such a way that you stick out and show the world what Jesus looks like

LESSON 9

SUPPLIES
A space large enough to play "Vanilla, Chocolate, Strawberry;" masking tape to divide the floor into sections to play the above game

READ: Philippians 3:17-20

ENGAGE
Twelve year-old Jeremy said he was a Christian and didn't mind telling his friends that he went to church and to youth group. However, during certain school days, he sure wasn't acting much like a Christian. He forgot his homework one day and asked to copy a friend's. Later, at lunch, some of his classmates were making fun of a new kid, and Jeremy joined right in.

Yes, Jeremy's *words* said he was a Christian, but his *actions* sure weren't saying that!

Someone once said, "Your actions speak so loudly that I can't hear what you are saying." That means it is *easy* to say, "I am a Christian, and I love Jesus," but words don't mean too much if our actions show something else.

ASK
How did Jeremy's words and action not line up?

Has someone ever said they liked you but then acted like they didn't? How did that make you feel?

If we say we love Jesus but act like we don't, how do you think that makes Jesus feel?

Why is it *not* good to say one thing and do another?

How are you doing at having your words match your actions?

DO
- Play a game of "Vanilla, Chocolate, Strawberry" with the kids
- To play create a rectangular space on the floor and divide it into three equal sections big enough for everyone who is playing to stand in
- Call one of the end spaces "Vanilla," call the middle space "Chocolate," and call the remaining space "Strawberry"
- Have everyone start in the middle (Chocolate) and explain the rules
- You will call out one word, either Vanilla, Chocolate, or Strawberry. Once you call it out, everyone must go to that space
- If someone goes to the wrong space, he is out. If you call the space everyone is in and someone leaves that space, he is out. If you are playing with multiple people, the last person into the called space is also out
- Play this game normally at first. Call out a space and have everyone move to it. You may even choose to point to that space for emphasis (and also help set up what comes next)
- After doing this for a bit, call out a space but point to a space other than the one you chose. For example, call out Vanilla but point to Chocolate
- Continue doing that for five or six calls

FOLLOW UP
Ask: Which was easier to follow me calling the spot and pointing to it or me calling the spot and pointing to another?

Move on to talk about how when our words and actions don't line up, it creates confusion. As Christians we need to make sure our words and actions line up, so no one is confused about what a Christian should be like

Ask: How should Christians be acting? At home? At school? With friends?

FINISH UP
- Pray and thank God for loving you even when you blow it
- Pray and ask God to help so everyone's words match their actions

LESSON 10

SUPPLIES
OPTION 1--Two flashlights, duct tape

OPTION 2--Two similar items—one that glows in the dark and one that does not

READ: 2 Corinthians 3:7 & 8

ENGAGE
Seven year-old Allie's family went on an awesome trip to the Great Wolf Lodge in the Pocono Mountains. One day, while at that enormous indoor waterpark, Allie saw someone with bright (and I mean bright) pink hair that was all spiked up.

Allie was taught not to stare at people, but she couldn't help but notice—in a sea of blondes, brunettes, and redheads, that pink hair really stood out! Even when Allie was fifty feet off the ground waiting to go down a huge waterslide, she could easily find that pink-haired person!

Did you know that as Christians, we, too, should stand out? People should take notice of us because we are living like Jesus. His love, His grace, His holiness, and His truth should shine through—even when we are surrounded by *lots* of people.

ASK
What did Allie see that really stood out?

What are some things that make you stand out?

In our Bible verses, what happened to Moses' face after he met with God?

Since we have the Holy Spirit in us, we should be glowing too! What does it mean for a Christian to "shine" or "glow"?

What are some ways you can shine out for Jesus?

DO—Option 1
- Grab two flashlights. Cover the "bright end" of one with duct tape or something similar
- Ask the kids, "If the power went out, which one would you want to use?"
- Smart-alecks aside, the kids will choose the one that actually creates a beam of light

DO—Option 2
- Have a regular Frisbee and a glow in the dark Frisbee (or you can use any item that comes in "regular" and glow in the dark—such as a ball, light saber, etc.
- Have the kids close their eyes then place both items in separate areas of the room, house, or church
- Turn out the lights and have the kids find both. It will be much easier to spot the glowing item in the dark

FOLLOW UP
Option 1--Ask: Why would you rather have a bright flashlight than a dull one?

Option 2--Ask: Why was it easier to find the glowing Frisbee (or whatever item it was) in the dark?

Discuss that our world is a dark place, but Jesus has called us to be bright lights. He needs us to live in such a way that we shine out for Him, not block His light by our attitudes, actions, etc. because people in our world need to see Him clearly in us

Finish by discussing how your family (class) can shine brightly for Jesus

FINISH UP

- Pray and thank God for all the people who are working to shine out for Him
- Pray and ask God to show each one where and how to shine out for Him

LESSON 11

SUPPLIES
Various flowers or sections of grass

READ: 1 John 2:24 & 25

ENGAGE
Six year-old Bobby got off the bus after kindergarten one day and started up the long driveway to his house. While walking, he noticed some beautiful blue and yellow flowers growing nearby. He thought his mom would really like them, so he pulled a couple out of the ground to take to her.

Mom was so excited to see that Bobby had brought her flowers! She put them on the kitchen table in a little water vase for everyone to see. However, by dinner time, those flowers weren't so pretty anymore. The blue and yellow petals were starting to curl in. By the next morning, brown spots were showing up. Bobby didn't understand what was happening, so Mom explained that flowers can only grow in soil. Once they leave the soil, they won't last very long.

As Christians, we are a lot like flowers. When we stay connected to Jesus, we can grow and grow. But when we separate from Him, well, we don't last very long.

ASK
What is your favorite color for flowers?

What lesson did Bobby learn about flowers?

What do our Bible verses say happens when we remain connected to Jesus?

What are things you can do to stay connected to Jesus?

How are you doing at those things?

DO

- If you have flowers in a flowerbed, take one out of the soil. If you do not have flowers, you can dig up a small section of grass (keeping the roots in the soil) and then pull out one or two blades of grass, while allowing the rest to stay in the soil
- If doing this with your family, compare the flowers in the soil (or blades of grass) with those not in soil over the next few days
- If doing this in a weekly classroom setting, you will need to prepare this a few days in advance. Remove a flower three days ahead of the class, another two days ahead of the class, and then one more the day before class. (Again, you can use grass as well)

FOLLOW UP

Ask: What do you notice about the flowers the longer they have been out of the soil?

Ask: Why do they get all withered like this?

Discuss how at first there didn't appear to be much of a difference. However, as time passed, it becomes very easy to distinguish between the ones connected to the soil and the ones *not* connected

Continue by stating that when we start to neglect the things that keep us connected to Jesus, it may not be noticeable at first. However, the longer we neglect those things, the easier it is to tell that we are "disconnected"

FINISH UP

- Pray and thank Jesus for being able to help you grow
- Pray and ask God to help each of you to stay connected to Jesus

LESSON 12

SUPPLIES
128 pieces of candy (M&M's, Skittles, etc) or 128 pennies, beans, or other such small item

READ: John 14:1-6

ENGAGE
"NO ADMITTANCE WITHOUT A PARENT OR GUARDIAN" said the sign at the park entrance.

Ten year-old Sarah and eight year-old Billy were crushed. They passed this park every day to and from school, and it looked like an awesome place to play. There were huge playgrounds, giant climbing walls, skate boarding ramps, bike trails, and more. All of that great stuff was waiting for them, but they couldn't get to it without a parent!

Rushing home, they asked their mom to *please, please, please* take them to the park. Thankfully for Sarah and Billy, Mom had time to do it. So, after dinner, the three went to the park and had a great time!

I'm sure you know that there are some places that children can only go if an adult is with them. But did you also know that you need Someone to be with you if you want to get into Heaven? The only way anyone is getting into Heaven, whether kid or adult, is if Jesus is with them!

ASK
What could Sarah and Billy do only if a parent was with them?

What are some things you are only allowed to do if an adult is with you?

What do our Bible verses say is only possible because of Jesus?

How can you thank Jesus for this?

Who can you tell about Jesus, so those people can go to Heaven too?

DO

- Have 128 pieces of candy ready (M&M's, Skittles, Hershey Kisses, etc.). If you do not have candy, you can use 128 pennies (or other coins)
- Pull out one piece and explain that the piece represents one person who goes and tells someone about Jesus
- Pull out a second piece and share that there are now two people who believe in Jesus, and they both go out and each tells another person
- Grab two more pieces so that you have four. Continue by letting your children know that these four went off and each told another person about Jesus
- Pull four more pieces out so that you have eight. Keep doing this through 16, 32, and then 64
- When you get to 64, say they all went out and told another person about Jesus. Dump out the rest of the pieces and say, "Now 128 people believe in Jesus and will be in Heaven."

FOLLOW UP

Go on to discuss with your family (class) how those 128 all started with just one person who told someone else about Jesus

Brainstorm ideas about how your family (class) can tell others about Jesus

FINISH UP

- Pray and thank Jesus for all the great things He has done for you
- Pray and ask God to use you all to tell others about Jesus

LESSON 13

SUPPLIES
One piece of paper for every child, a graphite pencil for every child

READ: Psalm 63:1-5

ENGAGE
Allison was hiking with her dad one hot Saturday afternoon when both realized that they forgot to bring any water. Unfortunately, they were already over a mile into their hike when they discovered this, so it was going to be a looong walk back.

Sweating like crazy and very thirsty, Allison and her dad finally made it back to the trailhead where a water fountain and vending machines were located. Even though she was dead tired, Allison bolted as fast as she could for the water fountain and took a nice long drink. It was the best water ever!

The Bible says that just as Allison *really* wanted water, so we should really want God. As Allison stopped to take a nice long drink, so we should stop every day and spend a good bit of time with the Lord by praying and reading the Bible.

ASK
Why was Allison really thirsty?

Can you think of a time when you were really thirsty? When was it?

Just like you really wanted a drink when you were thirsty, how can you tell that the writer of our Bible verses really wanted to spend time with God?

Do you spend time with God? What do you do during that time?

Is there more you could do to spend time with God?

DO

- Give each child a blank piece of paper and a pencil
- Have them press down hard with the pencil and write the word "GOD" in big, thick, and dark letters (those instructions will be important for the next step)
- After they have done so, have them rub their fingers across the letters. This should cause them to have considerable graphite residue on their fingertips

FOLLOW UP

Talk about how spending time with people causes them to rub off on you

Ask: We spend a lot of time with our family, can you think of ways your family all acts the same, uses the same phrases, etc?

Note that when we spend time with God, we give the Lord a chance to rub off on us. That means the more time we spend with God, the more we will become like Him! This is why it is important that we pray, read the Bible, attend church, sing worship songs, hang out with Christian friends, and much more.

FINISH UP

- Pray and thank God for wanting to spend lots of time with His children
- Pray and ask God to bring you all closer and closer to Him

LESSON 14

SUPPLIES
A space to do some exercises

READ: 1 Timothy 4:7-12

ENGAGE
During the 2016 Summer Olympics, America led the way winning 121 medals! Of those 121 medals, 46 were gold medals—which was also more than any other country! Way to go U.S.A!

Do you think it is easy to win a gold medal? Do you think any of those USA gold medal winners won because they *never* trained? Do you think any of those who won our 121 medals woke up a week before the Olympics and said, "I think I will try out for the Olympics today"?

No way! That didn't happen. To be an Olympic athlete you need to train hour upon hour, day upon day, for year upon year. It takes a *lot* of time and effort.

It is the same in our relationship with God. We *cannot* do any work to save ourselves from sin. Only the Lord can do that, but it does take time, work, and effort to grow in our relationship with Him.

ASK
What does it take to be an Olympic athlete? (Check out this article HERE to see what three Olympic athletes did to prepare)

What is something that you spend a lot of time working to get good at? (A sport, a hobby, a game, a subject in school?)

What are the things you do to get good at this?

What is Paul saying to Timothy in verses 7 and 8?

How are you doing at the areas listed in verse 12?

Where could you use some work to improve so your relationship with God can be *really* good?

DO
- Take your family (class) through an exercise regimen. Have them do some push-ups, jumping jacks, sit-ups, run in place, and more

FOLLOW UP
Ask: Exercise can be hard work, but why is it a great idea to exercise at least once a day?

Discuss how exercise is hard work, but it definitely helps our bodies be better, stronger, and healthier. From there, talk about how reading the Bible, doing devotions, praying, and more can be hard work, but it definitely helps our relationship with the Lord be better, stronger, and healthier

FINISH UP
- Pray and thank God for those in your life who are helping to train you to better know and love Him
- Pray and give the kids time to ask God to work on their weak areas

LESSON 15

Space to do a short race. Spoons and cotton balls (or ping-pong balls) for each child

READ: 2 Timothy 4:5-8

ENGAGE
Did you know that the Olympics started over 2700 years ago in Ancient Greece? As far back as 776 BC, people gathered for the Olympic Games. Some of the events included: foot racing, boxing, wrestling, discus, and javelin throwing. These events are still done today!

One event that is not done today is this interesting race. Each of the participants had to run with a lit torch in their hand. The winner of the race was *not* the runner who finished first. No, it was the runner who finished first--with his torch still lit. The race wasn't about going as fast as possible. The race was about taking each step in such a way as to finish with success.

Today, as Christians, we have a race to run. That race is called life. Again, it is not about finishing fast. It is about running each step well so that we finish with success!

ASK
How long have the Olympics been going on?

What were some of the sports from the first Olympics?

Do you like sports? If so, which one is your favorite? Why?

How did Paul say he was doing at running the race of life?

What is the prize for winning this race?

How are you doing in this race?

DO
- Set up a race for the kids. Have them run from one place another. The first person to the finish line wins. (You may also choose to do this as a relay race)
- Set up a second race for the kids. This time place a cotton ball, or ping-pong ball, on a spoon and see who can be the first person to get from one place to another *without* the cotton ball, or ping-pong ball, falling off the spoon

FOLLOW UP
Ask: Which race was easier? Why?

Discuss how the Christian life is like the second race not the first. As Christians we have to take careful steps to make sure that we successfully get to the end of each day having honored God in all we said, thought, and did

FINISH UP
- Pray and thank God for all that He has done for you and your kids
- Pray and ask God to help each child run the race of life well

LESSON 16

SUPPLIES
Backpack, weights or rocks

READ: Luke 10:38-42

ENGAGE
In Greek mythology, there was a guy named Atlas. It was his job to hold up the world. With his big muscles straining and working, the Greeks said that he spent his life laboring to keep the earth from falling. Meanwhile, the Bible says that God easily holds the whole world in the palm of his hand.

If Atlas were a real person, we would probably go over to this poor guy and say, "Hey, Atlas, why are you spending so much time and effort trying to hold up the world? Don't you know that God can take care of this without any problem at all?"

Today, many people are actually like Atlas. Their lives have problems, issues, struggles, hurts, and more, and they are working to handle them all alone. It seems like we should say to them, "Stop spending so much time and effort trying to handle all your struggles by yourself. Give them over to God. He can handle those problems so much better!"

ASK
What was Atlas trying to do all by himself?

What could you tell Atlas to help him out?

What kind of problems do you have right now?

In our Bible verses, what was Martha so worried about?

What does Jesus tell her?

Are you more like Martha, worrying about a bunch of stuff? Or are you more like Mary who was focused on Jesus instead of her problems?

Why is it better to be like Mary?

DO
- Load up a book bag with rocks or weights and have the kids go around a room, or up and down the steps, a couple times with it on their back (as you stand near them so they don't fall)
- Take the book bag off and have them retrace their steps

FOLLOW UP
Ask: Which way was easier—with the backpack or without it? Why?

Discuss how we can choose to go through life carrying all of our problems or we can give them all over to Jesus to carry for us

Have the kids think about some of their issues and problems as you prepare to finish in prayer

FINISH UP
- Pray and thank Jesus that He can take care of all your problems and struggles
- Pray and have the kids give God their problems and struggles

LESSON 17

SUPPLIES
A "treasure" such as a bag of candy, a map to find the treasure

READ: Proverbs 3:5-7

ENGAGE
Every year, when fall rolls around, you may start to hear a lot about corn mazes. Corn mazes, for those who don't know, are great big mazes cut into huge cornfields. Now, some people can get through a corn maze pretty easily in just a few minutes, others wander around lost for hours.

Usually, the people who use the map provided by the maze workers do *a lot* better! Those who try to find their way out all by themselves often end up very frustrated. They hit dead ends, or they go around in circles ending up in the same place they were half an hour earlier.

Life can be a lot like a corn maze. If we try to go through life trusting in ourselves to get through, it usually ends up pretty bad. However, if we trust in God and use His map (the Bible and His Spirit), life goes *much* smoother!

ASK
Have you ever gotten lost? How did it make you feel?

According to our Bible reading today, if you want to find the right path to walk in life, what must you do?

What do you think it means to "trust in the Lord with all your heart"?

How can you show that you trust in the Lord with all your heart?

DO

- Hide something you know the kids would like (such as a bag of candy) in a place that is virtually impossible to find. Tell the kids to search for it
- After some time has passed, provide a map that you have made to the location of the item

FOLLOW UP

Ask: How come you were able to find the candy with the map, but you couldn't find it without the map?

Discuss with the kids how the Bible is like our map for life. As it was much easier to find the candy with the map, so it is much easier to go through life when we consult God's map, the Bible, every day

FINISH UP

- Pray and thank God that He is trustworthy
- Pray and ask God to help each of you trust Him with all your heart

LESSON 18

SUPPLIES
A sheet of paper that states "Problem Solved!"

READ: Judges 6:11-16

ENGAGE

Little four year-old Johnny had a problem. His Styrofoam glider was caught in some tree branches about eight feet off the ground. No matter how hard Johnny tried to climb that tree, his muscles were not strong enough to pull him up. And no matter how high Johnny tried to jump, his little legs could not get him to that branch.

Yes, by himself, Johnny could do nothing about the glider. But then Dad came home from work and lifted Johnny onto his shoulders allowing him to easily reach up and grab the prized toy.

Did you know that God works just like Johnny's dad? Just because we are too little or too weak, that doesn't mean God is! The Lord is strong, and He is with us ready to lift us up and strengthen us to reach for the highest goal and handle the biggest jobs!

ASK

What happened to Johnny's plane?

If you got a toy stuck high in a tree, how would you get it out?

What big job did God give to Gideon?

How did Gideon reply in verse 15? What did God say back to him?

What do you need to remember when you think you are too small, too young, etc.

to handle a situation?

DO

- Tape a sheet of paper to the wall that says, "Problem Solved!" Make sure that the paper is well above the arm's reach of your tallest child when jumping
- Instruct your children to get the paper without using any object to assist them
- After it proves impossible, offer to lift a child up to grab it

FOLLOW UP

Discuss how we cannot solve many of life's problems on our own. We need God to help us. When we ask Him, He gives us the strength necessary to solve the problem or manage our way through it

FINISH UP

- Pray and thank God for promising to be with you all
- Pray and ask God to remind everyone that they are not alone in life

LESSON 19

SUPPLIES
Wordless bracelet supplies: Leather or suede lace and specifically colored pony beads

READ: 2 Timothy 2:25,26

ENGAGE
Have you ever heard the TRUE story of the flying turtle? Well, in southern California, some mean person thought it would be funny to duct tape a turtle to a bunch of helium-filled balloons and send it flying. And fly off the poor turtle did.

The helpless little guy flew hundreds of feet in the air for miles before a wind gust blew the balloons (and our shell-shocked friend) into a tree. Tangled in the tree for several hours, the turtle struggled to free himself...but could not. Finally, someone spotted him in the tree and called the Fire Department which came and set him loose.

Now, just like that mean person duct taped our poor, green buddy and left him trapped in a tree, so Satan likes to "tie up" people and leave them trapped in sin. But we know who can set them free. Jesus can. We don't need to be super-smart, super-talented, or super-anything to let people know this. We just need to care enough to tell them that Jesus can set them free.

ASK
What happened to that poor little turtle?

What would you do if you saw a turtle stuck up in a tree?

What do our Bible verses say Satan has done to people? How does he do this?

What do our Bible verses say we should do about this?

Who are some people that you know need Jesus to set them free from sin?

DO

- Want to check out pics and a video about the duct-taped turtle? Type in "duct taped turtle in tree" into an internet search engine
- Make salvation bracelets with leather or suede lace and black, red, white, green, and yellow pony beads
- Give each child one lace and have them tie a knot about one third of the way up the lace
- Provide the black bead first and explain that this represents our sin which keeps us from Heaven and out of a relationship with God. Have the children place the bead on the lace so that it butts up against the first knot
- Next provide the red bead and explain how this bead represents Christ's blood shed on the cross to pay for our sin. Let the children place this bead on their lace so that it butts up against the black bead
- The white bead comes next. Explain that when we accept Jesus as God's Son, who died for our sins and rose again, then we can be forgiven and our sins washed away. Have each child put the white bead on so that it butts up against the red one
- Second-to-last is the green bead. Let the children know that once we accept Jesus we need to grow in our relationship with Him. Just like plants and trees grow, so we need to grow closer to Jesus each day. Have the children place this bead on the lace next to the white one
- Finally provide the yellow bead. Explain that his bead represents Heaven. With Jesus in our hearts, we can be sure that when we die we will go to Heaven and be with the Lord and all other Christians forever
- After all the beads are on the lace, have each child tie a second knot up against the yellow bead, effectively locking the beads in place.
- Once that is accomplished, thread both ends of the lace through two clear or blue beads and tie in place.
- For a picture of the final product, check Appendix - C

FOLLOW UP

Have the kids explain what each bead means. Allow them to practice sharing its meaning

Encourage them to explain what their bracelet means to those they mentioned during the "ASK" portion of the lesson

FINISH UP
- Pray and thank God for those who told each of you about Jesus
- Pray for those that were mentioned in the ASK portion of the lesson. Ask God to work in their lives

LESSON 20

SUPPLIES
None

READ: Matthew 28:18-20

ENGAGE
At the beginning of July, 9 year-old Billy learned that his mom was going to have a baby, and he was going to be a big brother. He was so excited about this that he told everyone he could think of. He went all over the neighborhood telling his neighbors. He also told a ton of friends, and he even called relatives who lived far way to give them the news.

A couple weeks later, at Vacation Bible School, Billy learned about Jesus. When he learned about how Jesus died for His sins and rose again, Billy decided this was his time to accept Jesus as his Lord and Savior.

His parents expected Billy to tell lots of people, but to their surprise he didn't tell hardly anyone. This caused Dad to ask, "How come you were so willing to tell people about becoming a big brother, but you're not so willing to tell people you have become a child of God?"

ASK
What exciting news did Billy share with everyone?

What exciting news did Billy NOT share very much?

What is the most exciting news you've ever received?

Why do you think Billy was more interested in telling people about being a brother than about being a Christian?

What do our Bible verses say we should do?

How is telling people about Jesus really no different than telling people anything you are excited about?

DO
- Roll play with the kids. Tell them that you are a friend of theirs that does not know Jesus. What should they say to you? How could they help you learn about Him?

FOLLOW UP
After they have shared with you, offer some pointers, tips, and other information as needed.

FINISH UP
- Pray and thank Jesus for dying on the cross for everyone's sins
- Pray and ask God to help all of you tell others about what Jesus did

LESSON 21

SUPPLIES
A space to play Simon Says

READ: Joshua 24:14-15

ENGAGE

11 year-old Angela accepted the Lord when she was 7 years-old. So for the past four years, she has been telling people all about Jesus. In fact, unlike Billy from an earlier lesson, Angela is not afraid at all to tell people about Jesus. She has told friends, kids at school, neighbors, and just about anyone she could think of!

Now, while Angela doesn't have any problem using her *words* to talk about Jesus, she does have some problems with her *actions*. In fact, she is known to lie to cover up her mistakes. She has been caught cheating on a couple tests, and once even told her parents that she was going to see a Rated-PG movie with friends but then snuck into a Rated-R movie instead. So, while Angela's words say one thing, her actions say something else.

ASK

Why is it important for your words to match your actions?

How did Angela's words *not* match her actions?

In our Bible verses for today, Joshua is telling all the people that if they are going to serve the Lord, they need to *choose* to actually do it, not just say they will. If Joshua told you this today, what would you tell him back?

Do your words always match your actions? If your answer is "No," what can help you do better?

DO

- Play *Simon Says* with the children
- Start by playing the game normally. That is, have your words and actions line up. For example, say, "Simon Says touch your nose" then touch a finger to your nose
- After playing this way for five or six things, start to play so that your words and actions do *not* match up. For example, say, "Simon Says touch your toes" but you touch your knees instead
- Do this several times with various body parts or various actions

FOLLOW UP

Ask: Which was easier, the first way we played or the second way?

Ask: Why was the second way harder?

Discuss how it is important for our actions and words to match up. Otherwise, it can cause people to confuse what it means to be a Christian, which doesn't please God very much

FINISH UP

- Pray and thank Jesus for His great love for all of you
- Pray and ask God to help each child's words match his or her actions

LESSON 22

A series of "What Would Jesus Do?" questions

READ: Daniel 1:6-19

ENGAGE
One day, Cale and his friend Rio were alone at Cale's grandparents' house. While they were flipping through the channels, they came to a really bad show. Cale thought about quickly changing the channel because he knew the show was bad and Jesus wouldn't want him filling his heart with that stuff. However, Rio really wanted to watch it. Afraid of looking nerdy to his friend, Cale decided to watch the show.

Meanwhile, Stephen was at a campground with his parents. While playing with a group of kids there, one of them suggested that they all check out a website with bad stuff on it. Stephen knew that this was *not* a good idea, so he walked away.

ASK
Who did a better job of doing what was right? Cale or Stephen?

Why did Stephen do a better job?

Do you think it is hard or easy to say "NO!" to your friends when they want to do something that is wrong?

In our Scripture today, what did Daniel do when asked to do something wrong?

How could you tell that Stephen is more like Daniel than Cale?

Standing for Jesus and making choices that please Him is not always easy. How are you doing at this?

DO

- Go through some "What Would You Do If…" scenarios with the kids. See how they answer each one and provide feedback, correction, and/or praise as necessary
- What would you do if you were offered drugs?
- What would you do if a friend kept using curse words?
- What would you do if you were at a sleep-over and an inappropriate movie came on TV?
- What would you do if someone wanted to show you something bad on the internet?
- What would you do if you saw a classmate stealing something?
- What would you do if some of your friends were teasing someone?

FOLLOW UP

Feel free to come up with some scenarios of your own

Make sure to help your kids know what Jesus would have them do in each situation

FINISH UP

- Pray and thank Jesus for standing up for the whole world and being willing to die on the cross, so that everyone could be saved
- Pray and ask God to help each one of you stand for Jesus and His truth

LESSON 23

SUPPLIES
OPTION 1--Ingredients to bake cookies, brownies, or something else that is quick and easy

OPTION 2--Blank greeting cards or paper to be folded into cards, a list from your pastor with the names of people in the hospital, in nursing homes, and/or shut-ins

READ: Ephesians 2:1-10

ENGAGE

Listen to the true story of John Jenkins. He was a mean, angry man who hated God, Jesus, and all Christians. Every time his neighbors, the Mason's, tried to invite him to church, he would curse at them and tell them to "Keep your religion to yourself!" In fact, he made life hard for the Mason's in many ways even going so far as to shoot their dog with a BB gun whenever it came onto his property.

Yet, when John and his wife got into a car accident, and both of them were laid up in the hospital, it was the Mason's who collected their mail, mowed their lawn, watered their bushes, and took care of their house.

Moved by all that love and kindness, John and his wife started visiting the Mason's church after leaving the hospital.

ASK

What nice things did the Mason's do for Mr. Jenkins and his wife?

Can you think of a time when you did something nice for someone who had been mean to you?

In our Bible reading, what were we all like according to verses 1—3?

What did God do for us anyway according to verses 4-6?

What can you do to thank God for His underserved love and kindness towards you?

DO—Option 1
- As a family (or class), bake some cookies, make brownies or *Rice Krispie treats*, and/or something else, then have the kids take them to friends and neighbors

DO—Option 2
- Get a list from your pastor of people in the hospital, in nursing homes, or shut-ins
- Have the kids draw or make cards for those people
- See that those cards are mailed out or hand delivered

FOLLOW UP
Ask: Why is it always a good thing to show love to people—even if those people are mean to you?

As a family (or class), brainstorm ways you can show love and bless friends and neighbors on a regular basis

FINISH UP
- Pray and thank God for His great love for the whole world even though we don't deserve it
- Pray and ask God to fill each child with His love and use them to bless someone else

LESSON 24

SUPPLIES
Internet access and a device that can show internet videos

READ: Matthew 6:31-33

ENGAGE
10 year-old Douglas loves baseball. He thinks about baseball almost all the time, watches every Philadelphia Phillies game he can, and is outside practicing whenever the weather is nice enough—and sometimes when the weather isn't so nice!

9 year-old Alena loves soccer. She even used her own allowance money to buy a soccer ball and a mini-net. She spends most of the week anxiously waiting for her Saturday soccer game. And if she is not anxiously waiting for her *next* soccer game, she is excitedly talking about her *last* soccer game.

Zach Hunter loves Jesus. At age 12, he started a group called "Loose Change to Loosen Chains" to raise money to stop modern day slavery. During his teen years, he wrote three books and travelled the country talking to thousands of teenagers about following Jesus and being used to make a difference in the world.

ASK
We just read about what some kids and teens really love. What are some things that you really love?

What does Jesus say you should focus on and love more than anything else?

Do you love Jesus more than anything else?

What are ways that you can show Jesus that you love Him?

What is something you can do this week to show Jesus' love to someone else?

DO

- Show the kids this video about Zach Hunter. Go to youtube.com and type in "Here and Now – Zach Hunter"
- You may also like this video about 12 year-old Evilyn. Go to youtube.com and type in "100 Millionth Shoe Box Journey Begins - Evilyn Pinnow"

FOLLOW UP

Discuss how children and teens CAN make a difference no matter how young they are

Brainstorm ways that they, and you, can be difference makers for Jesus

FINISH UP

- Pray and thank God for the people who show Jesus' love to each of you
- Pray and ask God to help all of you focus on Jesus above everything else and be used by Him to make a difference in this world

LESSON 25

SUPPLIES
None

READ: Hebrews 11:1-7

ENGAGE
Imagine that your dad told you that he believed it was going to be cloudy and 25 degrees, but then he changes into his bathing suit, grabs some suntan lotion, and heads outside. Would you really believe what he just told you about the temperature?

What about this? Imagine a friend tells you that you are his best friend in the whole world, yet this "friend" never wants to spend any time with you. Would you believe this person really wants to be your best friend?

How about this one? Someone tells you that she is a Christian and loves Jesus with all of her heart. Yet, she never goes to church, likes to use swear words, and thinks reading the Bible is a waste of time. Would you believe her?

It seems pretty simple, doesn't it? If someone says something, you expect it to be backed-up by actions. Guess what? God is the same way. He wants to see our faith in action!

ASK
Do your actions always match your words?

Can you think of a time when someone's actions didn't match their words?

How did Abel, Enoch, and Noah *show* that their faith in God was real?

How are you showing that your faith in God is real?

Are there any areas of your life that need some work? If so, which areas?

DO
- Play a game of charades with the kids, giving each child a chance to act out a couple different things

FOLLOW UP
Discuss how in charades you have to *show* people, without using words, what you are. Likewise, as Christians, we have to *show* people we are Christians by our actions and attitudes

Ask: What should Christian actions and attitudes look like?

FINISH UP
- Pray and thank God for those who really *show* their faith
- Pray and ask God to help each child show their faith

LESSON 26

SUPPLIES
A children's story book that you are sure the kids are not familiar with

READ: Isaiah 65:1& 2

ENGAGE
10 year-old Bobby figured, since he had grown up in church and was now double-digits in age, that he had God all figured out. Because of this, Bobby didn't feel the need to pray or read the Bible anymore. He was making a *big* mistake.

Without talking to God on a regular basis, Bobby started making more and more choices that pleased him but did not please God. He stayed up late when his parents said to go to bed. He turned on cable channels and watched bad shows when his parents took their evening walk. He even stole a notebook off a classmate's desk, when he could not find his own.

It wasn't long before Bobby realized that he *did* need to spend time with God *every day*.

ASK
What bad decision did Bobby make in the story?

What other bad decisions did Bobby starting making because of that first bad decision?

How often do you talk to God in prayer and read the Bible?

What does God say about the people in our Bible verses who refused to talk to, or listen to, Him?

God is always reaching out wanting to hear from us and talk to us. When is a good time for you to talk to God every day and read His Word?

DO
- Ask the kids to try to explain something fun that happened today *without* talking
- Allow some of the children to give it a try
- Next, hold up a children's book (one you think no one in the class would know about) and talk about what a great story it has inside
- Ask one of the kids to tell you about the story
- When he or she replies, "How can I when I haven't read it?" move to the follow up questions

FOLLOW UP
Ask: Did you find that it was frustrating trying to share a fun thing that happened without using words?

Explain that this is how God feels sometimes. He wants to explain things to us, but He can't if we don't let Him talk to us in prayer

Ask: Is it possible to tell me about what's in this book if you haven't read it?

Talk about how the Bible is God's great story for our lives but we can't know that story unless we read it

Discuss with the kids the need for them to find time to pray and to read the Bible each day

FINISH UP
- Pray and thank God for always wanting to talk
- Pray and ask God to remind each of you to talk to Him throughout the day

LESSON 27

SUPPLIES
A deck of cards

READ: Exodus 3:1-10

ENGAGE
Do you wish you were a great and famous person? Do you wish you were the President of the United States, a powerful general, a star athlete, a famous actress, or a rich businessman?

Some people spend *a lot* of time daydreaming about being someone great. Some of those people even spend *a lot* of time working to make it happen. In the process though, they miss all the awesome things that God wants them to do.

It is possible that Moses spent his long days tending his flocks dreaming of being someone great. But I bet he never imagined God showing up to give him something great to do!

ASK
If you could be anything in the world, what would you be?

Do you think God wants you to spend a lot of time wishing to be something, or do you think He wants you to spend a lot of time praying and asking Him what you should be?

Why is it *more important* to ask God what He wants you to be and to do rather than trying to figure it out for yourself?

What great thing did God want Moses to do for Him?

In our Bible story, Moses was 80 years-old! That's very old! But whether you are very old or very young, that doesn't matter to God. No matter your age, God wants to do great things with you and through you. So what can you do to discover what God has for you?

DO—Option 1
- Get a deck of cards. Holding the cards face down, let the kids pick one. Take that card so that only you can see it. Have the kids make a couple guesses
- When they have guessed wrong a few times, tell them that they can ask you for some clues
- With the clues, they should be able to more easily guess the card

DO—Option 2
- State you are thinking of something in your head and have the children try to guess what it is. (Be sure to think of something your children would never guess)
- When it proves impossible to guess, move to a game similar to "20 Questions" and allow them to get clues from you

FOLLOW UP
Ask: Which was easier—when I gave you clues or didn't give you clues?

Talk about how much easier it is to ask God what we should do and be instead of trying to guess for ourselves

FINISH UP
- Pray and thank God for three things with which He has blessed you
- Pray and ask God to show all of you what He wants to do in and through you

LESSON 28

SUPPLIES
Red construction paper, markers, scissors

READ: 1 John 4:9 & 10

ENGAGE
Growing up without a mom and dad, Jonathan really doubted that anyone loved him. Sure, he had his Gramma, but he figured she *had* to love him. Filled with sadness and loneliness, Jonathan headed to church with his Gramma one Sunday. Seeing that Jonathan didn't look so happy, Pastor Rich asked to speak to him alone in the sanctuary after church. When the pastor asked the young boy what was wrong, Jonathan just cried and talked about how unloved he felt.

Pointing up at the cross on the sanctuary wall, Pastor Rich said these words, "Jonny, whenever you feel unloved, just look at this cross. There you can see just how much Jesus loves you. He loved you enough to die for you and your sins!"

ASK
Why was Jonathan sad?

Have you ever felt alone or unloved? When was it?

How do our Bible verses show us that we are always loved?

Do you think that knowing this will help Jonathan and others like him?

Who do you know that needs to find out how much Jesus loves them?

DO

- Have the kids trace TWO hearts onto red construction paper and then cut them out
- Inside both hearts have the children draw a cross as well as the words "Jesus Loves Me"
- If time permits, allow them to further decorate their hearts
- Tell the kids to keep one of these hearts next to their bed so they can remind themselves how much Jesus loves them
- Then tell the kids that they should give the other heart to someone who needs to know that Jesus love him or her

FOLLOW UP

Ask: Why is it always important to remind ourselves that Jesus loves us?

Sing the song, "Jesus Loves Me"

FINISH UP

- Pray and thank God for His great love for the whole world
- Pray and ask God to show each of you where you can share His love this week

LESSON 29

SUPPLIES
Clear glass, water, and food coloring

READ: Isaiah 1:18

ENGAGE
Everyone in the Smith family knew that "the white sofa" in the living room was *off-limits!* No kids were to sit on it, play on it, and definitely not eat on it. Yet, one day, 7 year-old Sarah thought she could sit on that sofa while putting on some of her mom's pink nail polish. That was a *big* mistake.

Not being careful enough, Sarah got a dime-sized smear of pink nail polish on the clean white sofa cushion! Trying desperately to clean it up with a wet rag, Sarah only smeared the stain across the cushion, making it ten times bigger!!!

Suddenly, Mom walked in and also tried to get the stain out. Yet, no matter what Mom did, the stain remained. Sarah thought her mom would hate her forever. But Mom informed Sarah that even though consequences were coming, she would always forgive her no matter how big the stain!

ASK
What did Sarah do that was a big no-no?

Have you ever stained something and the stain would not come out?

The Bible says that sin causes stains on our hearts, and we don't have the ability to get those stains out. But who can get them out?

Why is it great news that God can get out any sin-stain in our hearts?

DO

- Fill a clear glass with water. Gather the kids around and put one single drop of food coloring into the glass.
- As you all watch the single drop spread through the water, talk about how sin spreads in our hearts, causing all sorts of problems
- After sharing this truth, pour out the glass and refill it with fresh water
- You may also consider an illustration using water, coke, and bleach. To check it out, head to youtube.com and type in "You, Sin and the Christ - Simple Illustration"

FOLLOW UP

Have the kids list various types of sins in each of the three main categories of sin—thought, word, and deed

Discuss how the Bible says God gives us a new, clean heart when we accept Jesus and seek forgiveness for our sins

FINISH UP

- Pray and thank God that He has the power to remove any stain from our lives
- Pray and ask God to clean out the stains in your hearts

LESSON 30

SUPPLIES
Magnets, pennies (or dimes)

READ: Jeremiah 31:1-3

ENGAGE
There's a true story of young boy who started attending a church in Chicago during the 1800s. When his parents, who didn't go to church, moved to the other side of that large city, the young boy continued to attend that same Sunday school even though it meant a very long and weary walk each way. Someone asked him, "Why do you walk all that way when there are plenty of good churches closer to your home?"

The young boy replied, "Because they love a fellow over there."

Love was the magnet that drew the young boy to that church. This is kind of like our Bible verses for today which tells us that God "draws us to himself" with His great love.

ASK
Have you ever played with a magnet and a penny? What does the magnet do to the penny?

In our opening story, how was the love of the people like a magnet to the boy?

How is God's love like a magnet?

How can you be like a magnet with God's love?

DO
• Get a refrigerator magnet, or some other magnet you may have, and use

it to pull a single penny across the table. (Make sure to not have the penny actually touch the magnet)
- Keep adding pennies and see how many pennies the magnet can pull at one time
- You may consider purchasing some magnet rocks that work well with such experiments (and are just plain fun to play with!)

FOLLOW UP
Ask: How did the magnet do at drawing the pennies across the table?

Talk about how God's love is so great that it draws us to Him. And when we show God's love to others, it helps draw them to God

FINISH UP
- Pray and thank God for His great and "magnetic" love
- Pray and ask God to use each of you to show that love to others

LESSON 31

SUPPLIES
Sheets of paper or construction paper with big, bold words on them like "danger," "anger," "sin," "hurt," "pain," "bad TV shows," "bullies," etc

READ: Isaiah 45:11 & 12

ENGAGE
"You can't tell me what to do!" Yells 9 year-old Alex at his mom.

"Oh, can't I?" Mom asks, trying to keep her cool. "Listen, young man, I brought you into this world and I can take you out!"

It seems many parents have had similar conversations with their children. There is just something about us humans that doesn't like people telling us what to do. Children complain about their parents, and parents complain about their bosses.

Still, God knows life works best when we recognize authority and obey it. This is especially true when we recognize that God is our authority and our Creator, and we definitely need to obey Him.

ASK
What are some things your parents tell you to do that you do NOT like doing?

Do you ever complain about your parents or teachers telling you what to do?

Learning to obey our parents and other authority figures is good practice for obeying God, but what happens when we don't practice obeying others?

Why is it *not* a good idea to disobey your parents or God?

DO

- Place several sheets of paper on the floor with big, bold words on them like "danger," "anger," "sin," "hurt," "pain," "bad TV shows," "bullies," etc.
- After you have shown the children these papers strewn on the floor, put a blindfold on one and see if he or she can make it from one side of the room to the other without stepping on any. Offer no assistance
- After several children have gone through unsuccessfully, try again. This time be sure to guide each blindfolded child slowly through the papers step by step

FOLLOW UP

Ask: Which was easier—getting through with my help or without my help?

Ask: Why was it easier with my help?

Explain how parents know more than kids do. It is a parent's job to guide children through life, and it is a child's job to listen and follow

Go on to talk about how all of us, kids and parents alike, need to listen to, and follow, God because He knows more than anyone! And when we obey Him, life goes a whole lot better!

FINISH UP

- Pray and thank God for creating all of you, loving all of you, and giving all of you talents and abilities
- Pray and ask God to strengthen each child, so they can better obey their parents and Him each and every day

LESSON 32

SUPPLIES
None

READ: Jeremiah 29:10 & 11

ENGAGE
When 10 year-old Colin heard that his family was planning a trip to Mount Rushmore, he was incredibly excited. He couldn't wait to go. Unfortunately, though, the trip was six months away.

Each day, Colin would check the calendar and count down the days. It seemed like each day was taking weeks and the planned trip was never going to come. When the day finally came to leave for Mount Rushmore, Colin realized that all the waiting was worth it. He was now able to enjoy the vacation he had been anxiously waiting for.

You know, Colin waiting to go on his trip is similar to how we often need to wait for God's plans to happen. Sometimes, it takes patience to wait for God's promises. But it is always worth it!

ASK
What was Colin anxiously waiting for?

Can you think of a time when you had to wait awhile for something you really wanted? What was it?

In our Bible verses for today, how long would the Israelites have to wait before God would bring them home?

Why do you think that God wants us to learn patience and wait for His promises to be fulfilled?

DO

- Act all excited and tell the kids that you have the greatest story in the world to share with them
- When they are gathered around begin telling them a story, but share it as *slowly* as possible

FOLLOW UP

When the kids are visibly annoyed (and perhaps verbally annoyed as well!), ask: What's wrong with me telling the story like this?

Talk about how we like things to happen quickly, but God rarely works that way. Sometimes things, like great stories, take time. We have to be patient and wait

FINISH UP

- Pray and thank God that He always fulfills His promises
- Pray and ask God to give all of you the patience to wait for Him to fulfill His promises

LESSON 33

SUPPLIES
None

READ: 1 Peter 1:14-16

ENGAGE

The SR-71 fighter jet is one of the fastest fighters in the world. Travelling at speeds of over 2100 mph, it could fly around the entire earth in just 12 hours! Moreover, it can fly at an altitude of almost 85,000 feet. That is 17 miles high! It is such a high-powered fighter that it has broken more than 10 records! And for the bargain price of about 34 million dollars, one can be all yours.

Even though this fighter plane has so many awesome attributes, it is completely useless without a pilot. The plane can only fly effectively with a pilot at the controls guiding its every move. Likewise, we cannot do much either if we don't let God have complete control of our lives. Only when we let God be our pilot can we really soar!

ASK

What do you think would be the coolest thing about flying in a fighter jet going 2100 mph?

What do you think would be possible for you if you let God pilot your life?

Our Bible verses tell us that we must be holy as God is holy. What does it mean to be holy?

Do you think it is possible to be holy like God WITHOUT giving Him control of our lives?

DO

- Check out more information and pics of the SR-71 fighter online
- Have the kids pair up with a partner
- Have the partners stand face to face. One child will be the leader and the other will be "the mirror"
- The mirror must try to mimic any movement that the leader makes
- After a bit, switch who is the leader and who is the follower

FOLLOW UP

Say, "Right now we were just mirroring our friends, but in life we should try to be like a mirror of Jesus' life."

Go on to talk about how God is *The Most Good* in the whole universe. Because of this, He can best guide our lives to the most awesome things possible. We just need to follow Him to experience the holiest life possible

Ask: What are things we can do to learn more about how God wants us to live and act?

FINISH UP

- Pray and thank God for being great a pilot
- Pray and ask God to fly each child high into His holiness

LESSON 34

SUPPLIES
Various small objects

READ: Haggai 1:2-9

ENGAGE

One of your neighbors has 67 video games and 3 video game systems, and you don't have nearly that many. One of your classmates has an 83-inch TV in her house, and yours is not even half of that. One of your best-friends has a laptop computer, cellphone, I-pod and a ton of other cool stuff, and look at what you have. Hardly anything!

It is pretty easy to focus on all the stuff other people have, get jealous, and want all that stuff too. This is probably what happened to the Israelites in our Scripture for today. People were busy building big homes and gathering more and more stuff. This made everyone else want to do the same. Meanwhile, with a focus on "stuff," everyone forgot about God. Not good!

ASK

Do you ever get jealous of other people's stuff? If so, you are *not* alone. Can you think of an example of this happening?

Is it possible to focus on people's stuff and on God at the same time?

What did God say was happening to the Israelites because they were focused on stuff and not on Him?

What can help you focus more on God and the life He has for you?

DO

- Have one child stand in one corner of the room holding a relatively small object behind his or her back

- Have a second child standing in an opposite corner doing likewise with a different small object
- Tell the class to pay attention to both of the children at the same time (which is impossible) and then have each of the children in the corners simultaneously hold up their objects for just one second and then place them behind their backs again

FOLLOW UP

Ask: Were you able to see what both objects were at the same time?

Discuss how you could only focus on one of the objects at a time. To focus on one, you would need to stop focusing on the other

Talk about our need to take time out of each day to purposely stop focusing on the stuff all around us and to start focusing on God—with prayer, Bible study, devotions, etc.

FINISH UP

- Pray and thank God for loving each of you and having a great plan for your lives
- Pray and ask God to strengthen you all, so that you can follow that plan

LESSON 35

SUPPLIES
Two chairs of the same height

READ: Matthew 6:31-33

ENGAGE
10 year-old Richie was really struggling. He wanted to be a Christian and follow Jesus, but it seemed like all of his friends thought Jesus was for losers. He wanted to go to Sunday school and learn more about being a Christian, but it seemed like on the drive to church all his neighbors were outside playing. Because of this, he would have days when he worked to follow Jesus and other days when he just followed his friends.

Knowing his son was struggling, one day Dad sat Richie down for a talk and said these words, "Son, you are trying to sit on two chairs at once. If you try to sit on two chairs, you will fall between them. For life, you must choose one chair."

ASK
What do you think Richie's dad was trying to say when he told him to "choose one chair"?

When it comes to choosing who to follow in life, what does Jesus say about this in our Scripture for today?

How are you doing at following Jesus every day? At what areas are you doing well? What areas need work?

What will help you follow Jesus more and follow others less?

DO
- Place two chairs about 8-inches apart and have the children try to plant

their backsides on both chairs at once

FOLLOW UP
Discuss how difficult and uncomfortable it is to try to sit on two chairs at once

Move on to talk about how it is also difficult to try to live the life God has for us while struggling to focus on Him *and* the world at the same time

FINISH UP
- Pray and thank God for all that He can do in each child's life when they put Him first
- Pray and ask God to keep them focused on following Him all the days of their lives

BONUS LESSON

SUPPLIES
Button down shirt, shoes with shoe-laces, bread, peanut butter, knife, cup

READ: John 17:20-23

ENGAGE
Imagine that you wake up one morning to find that your left hand is completely gone and your right hand keeps slapping you in the face! That would be scary, annoying, and painful all at the same time! If one hand was missing from your body and the other hand kept hurting you, your life would not be that much fun. You would have a lot of trouble doing everyday things like buttoning a shirt, tying your shoelaces, and eating breakfast.

I hope this never happens to you, but did you know this happens in the "Body of Christ" all the time. The Bible says that all Christians make up Christ's body—which is the church. Sometimes Christians leave the church and the rest of the church must go on without them. And sometimes Christians do and say things that hurt the church and that isn't good either.

ASK
How do you think you would do trying to button your shirt or tie your shoes with just one hand?

It is hard to do normal things if the body is not working together. Jesus knows the church needs to work together too. So what did He pray for in our Bible verses?

What can be done, do you think, to help God's people stay close together and love each other instead of hurt each other?

DO
- Allow the children to try to button a shirt or tie shoes with one hand

- You may also consider having the kids see if they can spread peanut butter on a piece of bread with one hand or drink from a glass without using their thumbs

FOLLOW UP

Ask: How easy was it to do these things with just one hand?

Discuss how our body needs to work together to make things happen. Talk about how the Bible says the church is like a body and we all need to work together to help people know Jesus

FINISH UP

- Pray and thank God for providing a church for you all to attend
- Pray and ask God to guide each of you into a deeper love for Him, for fellow Christians, and for lost people

EPILOGUE

I hope God has truly blessed you as you have used this lesson book. I know He deeply desires to do so many awesome things in and through you. His plan for you, your family, and your ministry is truly remarkable! I trust you have grabbed hold of that.

If you, your family, or your class has been blessed in any way through these lessons, please do me the great favor of leaving a positive review on Amazon. Your review just may encourage another family to take this same journey.

I would also love to hear about what God has been doing through this lesson book in your home and/or classroom. Be sure to check my website www.markjmusser.com to contact me.

GOD BLESS YOU!

APPENDIX - A

APPENDIX - B

Printed in Great Britain
by Amazon

37937697R00051